ITA

Travel Guide

Discovering the Soul of Italy with essential tips for first-timers, Visiting: Rome, Venice, Florence, Naples, and much more.

Mike Steves

Copyright 2023

Table of Contents

Introduction

Italy is a beautiful country with rich cultural history, stunning architecture, art, and beautiful landscapes. It would help if you visited several places to experience Italy's soul truly.

This travel guide will explore top destinations, must-see attractions, and essential tips for first-timers.

Italy is a beautiful country in southern Europe known for its rich cultural heritage, stunning landscapes, and delicious food. It's home to the world's most famous art and architecture, including the Colosseum in

Rome, the Leaning Tower of Pisa, and the Vatican City.

In addition to its cultural attractions, Italy is also renowned for its stunning landscapes, including the beautiful Amalfi Coast, the rolling hills of Tuscany, and the rugged peaks of the Dolomites. Visitors to Italy can enjoy various outdoor activities, from hiking and skiing to swimming and sunbathing on the beautiful Mediterranean coastline.

Italy has a long and fascinating history, dating back to ancient times when it was known as the Roman Empire. Italy has influenced the world in fashion, cuisine, and design.

One of the highlights of visiting Italy is its delicious cuisine. Italian food is known for its fresh ingredients and is famous for pizza, pasta, and gelato dishes. Italian wine is also renowned worldwide, with regions such as Tuscany, Piedmont, and Veneto producing some of the world's best wines.

Overall, Italy is a country that offers something for everyone, from art and history enthusiasts to outdoor adventurers and food lovers. It's a must-visit destination for anyone looking to explore the soul of Europe.

Italy is also known for its vibrant and lively culture, with yearly festivals and events. The famous Carnival of Venice, held annually in February, is one of the world's most famous festivals, with participants donning elaborate masks and costumes for a week-long celebration.

Italy is famous for its fashion industry, with Milan being one of the world's fashion capitals. Visitors to Italy can explore fashion museums, attend fashion shows, and shop for designer clothes and accessories in the city's stylish boutiques.

Italy is a popular tourist destination, welcoming millions of visitors each year. Some of the best times to visit Italy are during the spring and autumn months when the weather is mild, and the crowds are smaller.

However, the summer months are also popular, with many tourists flocking to the country's beautiful beaches and coastal towns.

Italy has a well-developed transportation system, including a high-speed rail network that connects major cities such as Rome, Milan, and Florence. Traveling around the country by car or bus is easy, with many beautiful towns and villages waiting to be explored.

Italy has a rich history, stunning landscapes, delicious cuisine, and lively culture. From its famous art and architecture to its beautiful beaches and mountains, Italy is a must-visit destination for anyone looking to discover the soul of Europe.

CULTURAL HISTORY

Italy has a rich cultural history that spans thousands of years. Italy's cultural history is diverse and rich, and its contributions to art, architecture, music, and philosophy continue to influence the world today. Here are some key aspects of Italy's cultural history:

Ancient Rome: Italy was the birthplace of the Roman Empire, one of history's most powerful and influential civilizations. The ancient Romans made significant contributions to architecture, engineering, art, and philosophy, and many of their accomplishments continue to influence modern culture today.

Renaissance: The Renaissance began in Italy in the 14th century. It was a time of great artistic and intellectual growth, and Italy was central to this movement. The Renaissance saw the development of new artistic techniques, such as perspective and chiaroscuro, and the works of artists like Leonardo da Vinci, Michelangelo, and Raphael are still admired today.

Opera: Opera originated in Italy in the 16th century and has become an important part of Italian culture. Many of the world's most famous operas were written by Italian composers, such as Giuseppe Verdi and Giacomo Puccini.

Cuisine: Italian cuisine is known for its simplicity and use of fresh, high-quality ingredients. Many dishes now associated with Italian cuisines, such as pasta and pizza, originated in Italy.

Fashion: Italy is known for its fashion industry, and many of the world's most famous fashion designers are Italian, such as Giorgio Armani, Prada, and Gucci.

Art: Italy has a rich history of art, and many of the world's most famous artworks are located in Italy, such as the Sistine Chapel ceiling and Michelangelo's David statue.

Catholicism: Italy is the center of the Roman Catholic Church, and Vatican City, located in Rome, is the seat of the Pope.

Literature: Italy has a rich literary history, "The Divine Comedy" by Dante Alighieri is considered one of the greatest works of Italian literature. The works of Petrarch, Boccaccio, and Machiavelli are also highly regarded.

Architecture: Italy is known for its beautiful architecture; many of the world's most famous buildings and structures were built in Italy. Examples include the Colosseum and the Pantheon in Rome and the Basilica di San Marco in Venice.

Festivals and Celebrations: Italy is known for its vibrant festivals and celebrations, such as Carnevale in Venice and the Palio di Siena horse race in Tuscany. These events showcase Italy's rich cultural history and traditions and are important to Italian culture.

Music: Italy has a rich musical tradition; many famous composers and musicians hail from the country. Opera is an important part of Italian music, but Italy has also contributed to other genres, such as classical music, pop music, and electronic music.

Sports: Italy has a strong sports culture, and football is the most popular sport in the country. Italy has produced many famous footballers, such as Paolo Maldini and Francesco Totti, and has won four FIFA World Cups.

Italy's cultural history is diverse and multifaceted, encompassing various artistic, literary, culinary, and sporting traditions. These cultural contributions have significantly impacted the world and are celebrated and admired today.

FESTIVALS AND EVENTS

Italy has many vibrant festivals and events yearly, celebrating the country's rich cultural heritage and traditions. These festivals and events offer visitors a chance to experience the diverse cultural traditions of Italy and are an excellent way to immerse oneself in the country's history and heritage.

The most popular festivals and events in Italy:

Carnevale di Venezia: The Venice Carnival is a world-famous annual event in Venice, Italy. The event is known for its elaborate masks; visitors can enjoy parades, parties, and street performances.

Festa della Repubblica: Celebrated on June 2nd, the Festa della Repubblica is Italy's national holiday, commemorating the country's transition to a republic after World War II.

Palio di Siena: Held twice a year in the Tuscan city of Siena, the Palio is a horse race that dates back to the 17th century. Ten horses and riders representing different neighborhoods of Siena compete in the race, which takes place in the Piazza del Campo.

Festival of the Two Worlds: This annual festival takes place in the Umbrian city of Spoleto and features various music, theater, dance, and art events.

La Biennale di Venezia: The Venice Biennale is one of the world's most important cultural events, featuring exhibitions and performances from artists worldwide.

Feast of Saint Agatha: This religious festival is held annually in the Sicilian city of Catania to honor the city's patron saint. The festival includes a procession and a large feast.

Calcio Storico: This traditional game, also known as "historic football," is played annually in Florence and dates back to the 16th century. Teams representing the city's four historic neighborhoods compete in a violent and highly physical game that is a cross between soccer and rugby.

Festival Verdi: This annual festival celebrates the works of Italian composer Giuseppe Verdi and takes place in the composer's hometown of Parma.

La Notte Bianca: Held in many cities throughout Italy, La Notte Bianca is an all-night event featuring music, dance, and art performances.

La Festa della Rificolona: This festival is held in Florence on September 7th and is a celebration of the Virgin Mary's birth. Children parade through the streets carrying colorful paper lanterns, which symbolize the stars that appeared in the sky at the time of Mary's birth.

Festival dei Due Mondi: Held in the Umbrian city of Spoleto, this festival is dedicated to music, theater, and dance. The festival attracts artists from around the world and includes a range of performances and exhibitions.

Infiorata di Genzano: This flower festival takes place in Genzano, near Rome. The festival features elaborate floral arrangements made entirely of flowers and petals on the town's streets.

Festival of Sant'Efisio: This religious festival is held in the Sardinian city of Cagliari and features a procession of traditional costumes and horse-drawn carts.

Festival of Sanremo: This music festival is held annually in the Ligurian town of Sanremo and is one of Italy's most important music events. The festival features performances by Italian and international artists and includes a competition for the best song.

Festival delle Sagre: This food festival takes place in Asti in the Piedmont region and features a range of traditional Italian dishes and local wines.

Visitors to the country can experience the rich cultural heritage of Italy by participating in these events and celebrations.

FASHION

Italy is well known for its contributions to the world of fashion. The country has a long history of producing high-quality textiles and clothing, and many of the world's most famous fashion brands, such as Gucci, Prada, and Versace, are based in Italy.

Italian fashion is characterized by its attention to detail, use of luxurious fabrics, and emphasis on craftsmanship. Italian designers are also known for their innovation and creativity; many have significantly contributed to the fashion industry.

Milan, the capital of the Lombardy region, is the center of the Italian fashion industry. It hosts the world-renowned Milan Fashion Week, which takes place twice a year and attracts fashion buyers, designers, and enthusiasts worldwide.

The Italian fashion industry is also known for its contributions to the world of accessories, such as shoes, bags, and jewelry. Italian shoemakers, particularly, are highly regarded for their craftsmanship and attention to detail. Many of the world's top shoe brands, such as Ferragamo and Tod's, are in Italy.

Italian fashion is essential to the country's cultural identity, and its influence can be felt worldwide. Visitors to Italy can experience the country's fashion culture by exploring its many luxury boutiques and fashion museums or attending one of the many fashion events and shows throughout the year.

Another significant aspect of Italian fashion is its emphasis on traditional and classic styles. Italian fashion is known for its sophistication, with many designers drawing inspiration from the country's rich cultural history and heritage.

One example is the Italian tailoring style, characterized by its clean lines and attention to detail. Italian tailors are highly skilled craftsmen who take great pride in their work and often spend hours creating bespoke suits and clothing for their clients.

In addition to the high fashion world, Italy also has a thriving streetwear scene. Italian streetwear brands like Off-White and Stone Island are known for their edgy and urban styles, often incorporating bold graphics and bright colors.

Italian fashion is a diverse and dynamic industry encompassing various styles and aesthetics. Whether you are interested in luxury fashion or streetwear,

Italy has something to offer everyone, and the country's fashion culture will impress even the most discerning fashion enthusiasts.

CUISINE AND WINE

Italian cuisine is one of the world's most popular and beloved cuisines. It is characterized by its use of fresh, high-quality ingredients, simple yet flavorful dishes, and a focus on regional specialties. Some of the most popular Italian dishes include pasta dishes like spaghetti carbonara and lasagna, pizza, risotto, and various meat and seafood dishes.

Italian cuisine also includes a wide range of desserts, including gelato, tiramisu, and cannoli, all popular worldwide. Many Italian desserts feature creamy fillings, delicate pastries, and rich flavors, making them a decadent treat for anyone with a sweet tooth.

Regarding wine, Italy is one of the world's leading producers. The country is known for its various wine styles, from crisp and refreshing whites to bold and full-bodied reds. Some of the most popular Italian wine regions include Tuscany, Piedmont, and Veneto, each with unique styles and flavor profiles.

In addition to wine, Italy is also known for its various spirits, such as limoncello, grappa, and amaro. These spirits are often enjoyed as a digestif after a meal and are an important part of the country's culinary tradition.

Italian cuisine and wine are essential to the country's cultural identity and a major draw for tourists worldwide. Visitors to Italy can experience the country's food and wine culture by exploring its many restaurants, wineries, and local markets or attending food and wine festivals throughout the year.

It's also worth noting that Italy has several food and wine festivals throughout the year that celebrate the country's culinary heritage. One of the most famous is the annual Truffle Fair in Alba, which takes place from October to November and celebrates the region's truffle harvest. Other notable food festivals include the Cheese Festival in Bra, the Chocolate Festival in Perugia, and the Wine Festival in Montalcino.

Regarding wine, Italy is home to some of the world's most famous wine regions, including Tuscany, Piedmont, and Veneto. Visitors can take wine tours and tastings at many wineries throughout the country or enjoy a glass of wine with their meal at a local restaurant.

It's also worth noting that in Italy, wine is often served with food, and the two are meant to complement each other. Several regional dishes are specifically designed to be paired with certain wines.

For example, in Tuscany, the classic dish of bistecca alla Fiorentina (Florentine-style steak) is often served with a full-bodied red wine like Chianti.

Italy's cuisine and wine culture are important to the country's identity. Visitors can immerse themselves in this culture by trying traditional dishes, attending food festivals, and exploring the country's wine regions.

Italy is home to many food and wine festivals that celebrate the country's culinary heritage. Some of the most popular events include the Truffle Fair in Alba, which takes place in the Piedmont region every October and celebrates the prized white truffle, and the Salone del Gusto food and wine festival in Turin, which takes place every two years and features a wide variety of Italian and international cuisine.

Other popular food and wine festivals in Italy include the Chianti Wine Festival in Tuscany, the Barolo Wine Festival in Piedmont, and the Festa del Redentore in Venice, which features a spectacular fireworks display and traditional Venetian cuisine.

In addition to these festivals, Italy is also home to many food and wine tours, which allow visitors to explore the country's culinary traditions and taste some of its most famous dishes and wines. Visitors can take cooking classes, visit wineries, and sample local specialties in different regions nationwide.

RESTAURANTS AND BARS

Italy is famous for its food and wine culture, and plenty of restaurants and bars throughout the country serve delicious and authentic Italian cuisine.

In cities like Rome, Florence, and Venice, many high-end restaurants serve traditional Italian dishes like pasta, risotto, and seafood. These restaurants often have extensive wine lists and offer a fine dining experience.

However, plenty of casual and affordable eateries, including pizzerias, trattorias, and osterias, offer delicious food at reasonable prices.

In Naples, known for its pizza, many pizzerias serve the classic Neapolitan-style pizza. Visitors can also find many seafood restaurants along the coast serving fresh seafood caught that day.

In addition to restaurants, Italy has a vibrant bar scene, with many bars serving aperitivi, pre-dinner drinks, and cocktails. In cities like Milan and Florence, there are many trendy bars, while in Rome and Venice, visitors can find many historic and traditional bars that have been open for decades.

Italy has a rich culinary culture, and visitors can find various restaurants and bars to suit their tastes and budgets throughout the country.

TRANSPORTATION SYSTEM

Italy's well-developed transportation system makes it easy for visitors to travel. Italy's transportation system is efficient and affordable, and visitors have several options for getting around the country.

Here are some of the main transportation options:

Train: Italy's train system is extensive, efficient, and affordable. Trenitalia is the main operator, offering high-speed and regional trains that connect most major cities and towns. Tickets can be purchased online, at train stations, or from travel agencies.

Buses are a great option for traveling to smaller towns and villages not served by trains. Several bus companies operate nationwide, including Flixbus, Marino, and Baltour. Tickets can be purchased online, at bus stations, or from travel agencies.

Car rental: Renting a car is a good option to explore more remote areas of the country, but it's unnecessary if you're sticking to major cities and towns. Several car rental companies in Italy, including Hertz, Avis, and Europcar. It's worth noting that driving in some cities, such as Rome and Naples, can be challenging due to heavy traffic and narrow streets.

Taxi: Taxis are available in most cities and towns but can be expensive, especially for longer trips. It's best to agree on a price with the driver before starting the journey.

Bike: Biking is a popular way to explore some of Italy's cities, especially in smaller towns and villages. There are several bike rental companies, and many cities have bike-sharing programs that allow you to rent a bike for a short period.

Metro and buses: Italy's major cities have a public transportation system that includes metro and buses. Rome, Milan, and Naples have extensive metro systems that connect different parts of the city, while buses are a good option for getting around smaller towns and cities.

Trams: Some cities like Florence and Milan have tram systems that efficiently get around the city center.

Ferries: Italy has a long coastline and several islands, and ferries are a popular way to travel between different destinations. The main ferry operators in Italy are Tirrenia, Moby Lines, and Grimaldi Lines.

Air travel: If you're traveling long distances within Italy or to other countries, air travel is a good option. Italy has several international airports, including Rome Fiumicino, Milan Malpensa, Venice Marco Polo, and many smaller regional airports. Alitalia is the main airline, but several low-cost carriers, such as Ryanair and EasyJet, offer affordable flights.

A GONDOLA RIDE

A gondola ride is a traditional and romantic experience that is often associated with the city of Venice. Gondolas are traditional Venetian boats propelled by a single gondolier, using a long oar to navigate through the city's narrow canals.

You can admire Venice's stunning architecture and beautiful scenery from a unique perspective during a gondola ride. Gondola rides typically last around 30-45 minutes, and they can be booked from several different points around the city, including St. Mark's Square and the Rialto Bridge.

Gondola rides can be quite expensive, especially if you're traveling during peak tourist season. However, it's a once-in-a-lifetime experience that many visitors to Venice consider well worth the cost. If you're traveling on a budget, you can also opt for a shared gondola ride or a shorter ride that is less expensive.

A VAPORETTO

A Vaporetto is a water bus that's a great way to see the city differently. You can take a vaporetto along the Grand Canal or some of the city's more remote islands.

A Vaporetto is a waterbus that serves as a public transportation system in Venice, Italy. It is one of the main ways to travel around the city's various islands, as Venice is built on a lagoon and is mostly pedestrianized.

The Vaporetto is operated by ACTV, the public transport company in Venice, and it runs along the city's main waterways, including the Grand Canal. There are several different Vaporetto lines, each with its designated route and stops. The Vaporetto is an affordable way to get around Venice, with tickets costing a few euros per ride or a few dozen euros for multi-day passes.

While the Vaporetto is an efficient mode of transport, it can be crowded and busy during peak tourist season. It's also important to remember that the Vaporetto is subject to tides and weather conditions, so that services may be delayed or suspended in adverse conditions.

Nonetheless, a Vaporetto ride is a great way to experience the city's unique transportation system and see Venice from the water.

Overall, Italy's transportation system is well-developed, and visitors have several options for getting around the country, whether by train, bus, car, taxi, bike, ferry, or plane. It's important to plan your transportation ahead of time to ensure that you can get to your desired destinations efficiently and cost-effectively.

Rome

Rome is the capital of Italy. It's a city full of ancient ruins, museums, and churches that are a testament to its fascinating past.

Rome is one of the most popular destinations in Italy and the world. It's known for its incredible architecture, art, and ancient ruins. When visiting Rome, you must visit the Colosseum, the Roman Forum, and the Pantheon. You can also visit the Vatican City and the Sistine Chapel to experience some of the most beautiful art in the world.

One of the iconic landmarks in Rome is the Colosseum, which is an amphitheater that was built over 2,000 years ago. It was used for gladiatorial contests, public spectacles, and other events. Today, it's one of Rome's most visited tourist attractions and a must-visit for anyone interested in ancient history.

The Pantheon is another famous landmark in Rome, known for its impressive dome and stunning interior. This ancient temple was originally built in 27 BC and has been used for various purposes throughout its history, including as a Christian church.

The Vatican City, located within Rome, is also a must-visit location for anyone interested in art and history. The Vatican Museums are home to an incredible collection of art and artifacts, including works by Michelangelo, Raphael, and Botticelli. The Sistine Chapel, with its iconic ceiling painted by Michelangelo, is a famous attraction in Vatican City.

Rome is also known for its delicious food, including pasta dishes, pizza, and gelato. Some must-try dishes include carbonara (pasta with bacon and egg), amatriciana (pasta with tomato sauce and bacon), and cacao e pepe (pasta with cheese and pepper).

Rome is a city full of history, culture, and delicious food. Its ancient ruins, museums, and churches are a testament to its fascinating past, and its culinary scene is one of the best in Italy.

Rome has a rich and fascinating history, with many incredible sights and experiences. Whether you're interested in ancient Roman history, art, and architecture or simply soaking up the atmosphere of this beautiful city, Rome is sure to captivate and inspire you.

Rome is a city full of fascinating history, culture, and art. Here are some more things to see and do when visiting Rome.

Let's get started!

COLOSSEUM

The Colosseum is an ancient amphitheater located in the heart of Rome. It was built nearly 2,000 years ago and is one of Italy's most iconic landmarks. It was previously used for gladiatorial contests and public spectacles, and it's estimated to hold up to 80,000 spectators.

The Colosseum is one of Rome's most iconic landmarks and a must-visit for anyone interested in ancient Roman history. This impressive amphitheater dates back to 80 AD and was used for gladiator battles and other public spectacles.

The Colosseum, also known as the Flavian Amphitheatre, is an iconic symbol of Rome and one of the most visited landmarks in Italy. It is a massive oval-shaped amphitheater in the center of Rome, just east of the Roman Forum. The Colosseum was built in 70-80 AD and could hold up to 80,000 spectators who came to watch gladiatorial contests, public spectacles, and other events.

The Colosseum is an architectural marvel with its impressive network of arches, columns, and seating levels. Despite being partially destroyed by earthquakes and stone robbers over the centuries, the Colosseum still stands tall and is a testament to the ingenuity of the ancient Roman engineers.

Today, visitors can tour the Colosseum and learn about its fascinating history through audio guides, guided tours, or self-guided tours. Visitors can explore the underground tunnels.

If you're planning a trip to Rome, visiting the Colosseum should be on your list of things to do. Here's a travel guide to help you plan your visit:

Hours of Operation: The Colosseum is open every day except for Christmas Day and New Year's Day. The opening hours vary depending on the time of year, so checking the official website for up-to-date information is important. Generally, the Colosseum opens at 8:30 am and closes one hour before sunset.

Ticket Information: There are several different types of tickets available for the Colosseum, including standard admission, skip-the-line tickets, and guided tours. Purchasing tickets in advance is highly recommended to avoid long lines and ensure availability. You can purchase tickets online through the official website or third-party ticket vendors.

Guided Tours: If you're interested in learning more about the history of the Colosseum, a guided tour is a great option. Several tour companies offer guided tours ranging from one to three hours. Some tours may also include access to restricted areas of the Colosseum, such as the underground chambers.

Accessibility: The Colosseum is accessible to visitors with disabilities, although some areas may be difficult to navigate. Ramps and elevators are available, and guided tours are specifically designed for visitors with disabilities.

What to Bring: It's important to bring comfortable shoes, as much walking is involved. It's also a good idea to bring sunscreen and a hat, as much of the Colosseum is exposed to the sun. Finally, don't forget to bring a camera to capture the incredible views!

Nearby Attractions: The Colosseum is located in the heart of Rome, so there are plenty of other nearby attractions, including the Roman Forum, Palatine Hill, and the Arch of Constantine.

When planning a visit to the Colosseum, there are a few things to remember. First, purchasing tickets in advance is important to avoid long lines and ensure availability. Several types of tickets are available, including standard admission, guided tours, and special access tickets to areas not typically open to the public.

It's also important to dress appropriately for the weather and wear comfortable shoes, as there will be a lot of walking and standing involved. Visitors should also bring plenty of water and sunscreen during summer, as it can get hot and sunny.

Once inside the Colosseum, visitors should take the time to explore the different levels and sections, including the underground chambers where gladiators and animals were kept before fights. It's also recommended to visit the nearby Roman Forum and Palatine Hill, as these areas offer an understanding of the history and culture of ancient Rome.

Visitors should respect the site and follow all rules and regulations, including not touching or removing artifacts or structures. It's also important to be aware of pickpockets and other scams, especially in crowded areas.

Overall, visiting the Colosseum is a must for anyone traveling to Rome and offers a unique glimpse into Italy's ancient history and culture.

THE ROMAN FORUM

The Roman Forum is another must-see attraction in Rome, and it is just a short walk from the Colosseum. This ancient public square was the center of political and social life in ancient Rome and is home to several impressive ruins and monuments.

The Roman Forum, also known as the Forum Romanum in Latin, was the center of political and social activity in ancient Rome. It was the site of many important public buildings, including the Senate House, temples, and basilicas.

Today, the Roman Forum is a popular tourist destination and a UNESCO World Heritage Site. Visitors can see the ruins of many ancient structures, including the Temple of Vesta, the Arch of Titus, and the Temple of Saturn.

One of the best ways to experience the Roman Forum is by taking a guided tour, which can provide valuable historical and cultural context for the site. Visitors should also wear comfortable shoes, as there is a lot of walking involved, and be prepared for crowds during peak tourist season.

In addition to the Roman Forum, visitors should also consider visiting the nearby Palatine Hill, which was the site of the imperial palaces of ancient Rome. The Roman Forum, Palatine Hill, and the Colosseum offer a fascinating glimpse into Italy's ancient history and culture.

The Roman Forum is a must-see attraction for anyone interested in ancient history and culture. Here are some tips for visiting the Roman Forum:

Get there early: The Roman Forum can get crowded, especially during peak tourist season. To avoid crowds, try to get there as early in the day as possible.

Wear comfortable shoes: A lot of walking is involved in exploring the Roman Forum, so be sure to wear comfortable shoes. The terrain can be uneven, so be prepared for some rough terrain.

Consider a guided tour: A guided tour can provide valuable historical and cultural context for the site and help you navigate the complex layout of the Forum.

Bring sunscreen and water: The Roman Forum is an open-air site, so be sure to bring sunscreen and plenty of water, especially during the hot summer months.

Plan for additional time: The Roman Forum is a vast site with many important structures and ruins to explore, so spend several hours there to appreciate its history and significance fully.

Visit nearby attractions: The Roman Forum is located near several other important historical and cultural attractions, including the Colosseum and Palatine Hill. Be sure to visit these sites to understand ancient Rome comprehensively.

Several ticket options are available for visiting the Roman Forum, including combined tickets with the Colosseum and Palatine Hill and guided tours that include skip-the-line access.

It's important to note that strict rules regarding preserving the Roman Forum exist, and visitors cannot touch or climb on any of the ruins.

Additionally, smoking, eating, and drinking are prohibited within site.

THE PANTHEON

Another famous landmark in Rome is the Pantheon. It's a remarkable example of ancient Roman architecture and engineering and is considered one of the most well-preserved buildings from ancient Rome.

The Pantheon is in the heart of Rome, near Piazza Navona and the Trevi Fountain. The Pantheon was established in 126 AD as a temple to all the gods, and it's one of the best-preserved ancient Roman buildings. It was later converted into a Christian church in the 7th century.

The Pantheon is renowned for its stunning dome, which is made of concrete and is the largest unsupported dome in the world. The interior of the Pantheon is also breathtaking, with its marble floors, ancient statues, and intricate detailing.

The Pantheon is an ancient temple in the heart of Rome, Italy. The Pantheon features a large circular dome with a central oculus, or opening, that provides natural light to the interior. The dome is made of concrete and is still the biggest unreinforced concrete dome in the world. The temple's interior is also impressive, with its intricate marble floors, ornate decorations, and numerous chapels.

Today, the Pantheon is a popular tourist attraction and a functioning church. Visitors are free to enter and explore the temple during regular opening hours. Guided tours are usually available for those who want to learn more about the history and architecture of the building. It's important to note that visitors should dress appropriately and be respectful of the religious services that take place within the church.

Visiting the Pantheon is a must-do for anyone interested in ancient Roman history and architecture. It's a chance to see one of the most impressive and well-preserved buildings from ancient Rome and experience a unique history and culture.

The Pantheon is one of the most iconic buildings in Rome and a must-visit destination for anyone interested in history and architecture. Here's a travel guide to help you plan your visit to the Pantheon:

Admission: Admission to the Pantheon is free and open to visitors every day of the week except for some public holidays.

Best time to visit: The Pantheon is a popular tourist destination, so it's best to visit early in the morning to avoid crowds. It's also a good idea to visit on a sunny day to see the light shining through the oculus in the dome.

Other tips: When visiting the Pantheon, remember to dress appropriately and be respectful, as it's still a functioning church. You should also be aware that no public restrooms are available on site.

Nearby attractions: The Pantheon is located in a bustling part of Rome, and there are many other attractions to visit nearby, including the Trevi Fountain, Piazza Navona, and the Spanish Steps.

THE VATICAN CITY AND THE SISTINE CHAPEL

The Vatican City is another must-visit attraction in Rome, a city-state that's the headquarters of the Roman Catholic Church. The most famous attraction in Vatican City is the Sistine Chapel, famous for its stunning ceiling painted by Michelangelo.

Vatican City is the smallest country in the world and is located in the heart of Rome. It's a significant religious and cultural center and home to the famous Sistine Chapel.

Vatican City is an independent city-state located within Rome, known as the smallest country in the world. The Vatican is home to some of the world's most famous and important art collections, including the Sistine Chapel, a must-see for any art lover visiting Rome.

The Sistine Chapel is famous for its ceiling, which Michelangelo painted in the early 16th century. The ceiling depicts scenes from the Book of Genesis, including Adam's creation and man's fall. The chapel walls are also covered in frescoes by other famous Renaissance artists, including Botticelli and Perugino.

The Sistine Chapel is famous for its ceiling, painted by Michelangelo. The ceiling depicts scenes from the book of Genesis and is considered one of the greatest masterpieces of Western art. Visitors can also see other famous artworks in the Vatican Museums, such as the Raphael Rooms and the Gallery of Maps.

The Vatican Museums house a vast collection of art and artifacts throughout history, including sculptures, paintings, and tapestries. The museums are home to many famous works of art, including the Laocoön and his Sons, the Apollo Belvedere, and the Belvedere Torso. The museum's highlight is the Sistine Chapel, famous for its ceiling painted by Michelangelo.

St. Peter's Basilica is one of the largest churches in the world and is a masterpiece of Renaissance architecture. The basilica is home to many famous works of art, including Michelangelo's Pieta and Bernini's baldachin.

The Vatican Gardens are a tranquil oasis in the heart of the city, covering more than half of the Vatican City's area. The gardens feature fountains, sculptures, and various plants and trees. Visitors can take guided tours of the gardens to learn more about their history and design.

Vatican City is surrounded by walls built in the 9th century to protect the city from invaders. Visitors can walk along the top of the walls to enjoy stunning views of the city and the surrounding countryside.

When planning a visit to the Vatican City and the Sistine Chapel, it's essential to remember that it's a highly popular tourist destinations. It's recommended to book your tickets in advance and be prepared for long queues.

It's also important to note that the Vatican is closed on Sundays and some religious holidays. Visitors to the Vatican City can attend a Papal Audience, which takes place most Wednesdays when the Pope is in Rome. During the audience, the Pope addresses the crowd, blesses them, and meets with individual pilgrims. Tickets for the audience are free but must be reserved in advance.

The Vatican Museums and St. Peter's Basilica are open daily, except on Sundays and some religious holidays. Visitors can purchase tickets online or in person, but booking tickets in advance is recommended to avoid long queues. The museums and basilica have different opening and closing times, so visitors should check the official website for the latest information.

When visiting Vatican City, Men should wear long pants and shirts with sleeves, while women should wear dresses or skirts that cover their knees and shirts with sleeves. Visitors who do not follow the dress code may be refused entry to the museums and basilica.

Vatican City is a UNESCO World Heritage site. When visiting the Vatican City, visit St. Peter's Basilica, the Vatican Museums, and the Sistine Chapel.

It's important to note that Vatican City has a strict dress code and behavior rules, so read up on them before your visit. Additionally, many tour guides are available, so booking one in advance is recommended to get the most out of your visit.

Overall, visiting the Vatican City and the Sistine Chapel is a must-see for anyone visiting Rome. It's a beautiful historic site and a chance to experience some of the world's most famous art and architecture.

THE TREVI FOUNTAIN

The Trevi Fountain is in the Trevi district of Rome, close to the Piazza di Spagna and the Spanish Steps.

The fountain was designed by architect Nicola Salvi in the 18th century and completed by Giuseppe Pannini in 1762. The fountain features the god of the sea, Neptune, and his horses, as well as several other intricate details and sculptures.

It's a tradition to throw a coin over your left shoulder into the fountain, which is said to bring good luck and ensure a return trip to Rome. It's estimated that around 3,000 euros are thrown into the fountain daily!

This iconic Baroque fountain is one of Rome's most famous landmarks and a must-visit for anyone visiting the city. The fountain stands at the junction of three roads and is named after the Trevi district in which it is located.

The Trevi Fountain is known for its stunning Baroque architecture and grand scale. The fountain is made of travertine stone and contains a central statue of Neptune, the Roman god of the sea, riding a chariot pulled by two sea horses. The fountain is adorned with other mythological figures, such as tritons and sea nymphs.

One of the popular traditions at the Trevi Fountain is to throw a coin over your shoulder into the fountain. According to legend, throwing a coin with your right hand over your left shoulder will ensure a return visit to Rome. Throwing two coins will lead to a new romance while throwing three coins will lead to marriage.

The Trevi Fountain is open to the public 24 hours a day and free to visit. However, it can be crowded with tourists, so it's best to visit early in the morning or late at night to avoid crowds.

Here is a travel guide to help you plan your visit:

Crowds: The Trevi Fountain can get crowded, especially during peak tourist season. Visiting early in the morning or late at night is recommended to avoid crowds.

Nearby attractions: There are several other attractions located near the Trevi Fountain, including the Pantheon, Piazza Navona, and the Spanish Steps.

Dress code: It's important to dress modestly when visiting the Trevi Fountain, as it's considered a religious site.

Accessibility: The Trevi Fountain is accessible by public transportation, including buses and the metro. However, the area around the fountain is pedestrian-only, so wearing comfortable walking shoes is recommended.

THE SPANISH STEPS

The Spanish Steps, or Scalinata di Trinità dei Monti in Italian, is a popular landmark in Rome. It has a staircase of 135 steps leading up to the Trinità dei Monti church at the top.

The Spanish Steps are in the heart of Rome, near the Piazza di Spagna and the Via dei Condotti shopping district.

The Spanish Steps were built in the early 18th century to connect the Trinità dei Monti church with the Piazza di Spagna below. They were financed by the French diplomat Étienne Gueffier and designed by the Italian architect Francesco de Sanctis.

These elegant steps lead up to the Trinità dei Monti church and offer stunning views over the city. The Spanish Steps are a popular spot for tourists and locals alike and are particularly beautiful when the azaleas are in bloom.

The Spanish Steps is a popular tourist destination in Rome, located in the Piazza di Spagna. The steps were built in the 18th century and were designed by the architect Francesco De Sanctis. They consist of 135 steps that lead up to the Trinità dei Monti church at the top of the hill.

Visitors can enjoy the beautiful Baroque architecture of the Spanish Steps. The area surrounding the Spanish Steps is also home to many luxury shops, cafes, and restaurants.

The most popular times to visit the Spanish Steps is during the spring when the azaleas bloom, and the steps are decorated with flowers. Another popular time to visit is during Christmas, when the steps are decorated with lights, and a Nativity scene is set up at the base.

It's important to note that visitors should not sit or eat on the Spanish Steps, as local regulations prohibit it.

The Spanish Steps can get crowded during peak season. Visiting early in the morning or later in the evening is best to avoid crowds. You can sit on the steps and enjoy the views of the city or visit the Trinità dei Monti church at the top.

The Piazza di Spagna and the Via dei Condotti shopping district are nearby and worth a visit. You can also walk from the Spanish Steps to the Trevi Fountain and the Pantheon.

There are many cafes and restaurants around the Spanish Steps where you can grab a bite or drink. It's a great place to relax and people-watch.

The Spanish Steps are easily accessible by public transportation, and you can take the metro A line to the Spagna station or the bus to the Piazza di Spagna stop. If you're walking, it's a pleasant stroll through the narrow streets of Rome to reach the Steps.

THE CATACOMBS

Beneath the streets of Rome lie a network of ancient catacombs, where early Christians were buried. These underground tunnels offer a fascinating glimpse into Rome's early Christian history and are worth visiting.

The catacombs are a network of underground burial sites in Rome that were used primarily by early Christians as a place to bury their dead.

There are several catacombs in Rome, but the most famous and accessible ones are the Catacombs of

Domitilla, the Catacombs of San Callisto, and the Catacombs of Priscilla.

One of the most famous catacombs is the Catacombs of San Callisto, located on the Appian Way. This catacomb is home to over 500,000 graves and is one of Rome's largest and most well-preserved catacombs. Other notable catacombs include the Catacombs of Priscilla, which features some of the oldest Christian frescoes, and the Catacombs of Domitilla, which has an underground basilica and chapel.

Visitors to the catacombs can expect to see narrow underground passages, ancient tombs, and early Christian art. Some catacombs also have guides that provide information about the history and importance of the site. It's important to note that the catacombs can be quite cold and damp, so visitors should dress appropriately and wear comfortable shoes.

To visit the catacombs, it's best to join a guided tour or hire a private guide. Many catacombs are located outside the city center and can be difficult to access on public transportation.

Additionally, some catacombs have restricted access and require a reservation in advance. The catacombs in Rome are a network of underground burial sites dating back to the 2nd century AD, primarily used by Christians and Jews. These catacombs can be found outside the walls of Rome, as it was illegal to bury the dead inside the city limits.

Visitors to the catacombs can take guided tours to explore the maze of tunnels and chambers adorned with intricate frescoes, sculptures, and inscriptions. The tours are conducted in several languages, including English, and provide a fascinating insight into Rome's early Christian and Jewish communities.

It's important to note that the catacombs can be quite chilly, damp, and dimly lit, so it's recommended to wear warm clothing and sturdy footwear. Visitors should also respect the burial sites and follow the catacomb authorities' rules and regulations.

Overall, the catacombs offer a unique and intriguing glimpse into the history of ancient Rome and the early Christian and Jewish communities that lived there.

THE CITY'S PARKS

Rome has several beautiful parks and gardens that allow visitors to relax and enjoy the city's natural beauty.

Rome has several beautiful parks, including the Villa Borghese and the Gianicolo. These green spaces offer a peaceful escape from the bustle of the city and are a better place to relax and soak up the atmosphere.

Rome has several beautiful parks perfect for a leisurely walk or a picnic.

Here are some of the best parks to visit in Rome:

Villa Borghese: Rome's largest public park, covering over 200 acres, with beautiful gardens, a lake, and several museums. The park is home to several museums, art galleries, and theaters, as well as beautiful gardens, fountains, and sculptures.

Parco degli Acquedotti: This park is located on the outskirts of Rome and is known for its ancient Roman aqueducts and beautiful green spaces. Visitors can walk or bike along the aqueducts and enjoy the peaceful surroundings.

Villa Ada: This park is located in the north of Rome and is the second-largest public park in the city. It's a great place to go for a picnic, a jog, or a bike ride, and it's also home to several cultural events throughout the year.

Parco Savello (Giardino degli Aranci): This park is located on Aventine Hill and offers stunning city views. The park is known for its orange trees, and visitors can enjoy a leisurely walk or a picnic in the peaceful surroundings.

Villa Doria Pamphili: A peaceful park with beautiful gardens, walking trails, and a panoramic view of Rome. This park is located in the west of Rome and is the third-largest public park in the city. It's a great place to go for a hike, a bike ride, or a picnic, and it's also home to several historical buildings and monuments.

Parco della Caffarella - a large park with several walking and cycling trails, perfect for a day out in nature.

Piazza del Popolo - a beautiful square located in the heart of Rome with beautiful fountains, gardens, and an Egyptian obelisk.

Giardino degli Aranci - a small park on the Aventine Hill, known for its beautiful city views and orange trees.

These parks are beautiful and peaceful and offer a better opportunity to escape the hustle and bustle of the city and enjoy some nature.

Visitors to Rome should not miss the opportunity to explore these beautiful parks and gardens and experience the city's natural beauty.

Venice

Venice is a beautiful and unique city in northeastern Italy and is built on a group of 118 islands separated by canals and linked by over 400 bridges. It's known for its romantic atmosphere, beautiful architecture, and unique gondolas and water taxis transportation system.

Venice is a beautiful city located in the northeast of Italy, and it's known for its beautiful canals and architecture. When visiting Venice, you should take a gondola ride, visit St. Mark's Basilica, and explore the Rialto Bridge.

The most iconic landmarks in Venice are St. Mark's Square and Piazza San Marco. It's the largest square in Venice and is surrounded by beautiful buildings, including St. Mark's Basilica, one of Italy's most beautiful and important churches.

Another must-visit attraction in Venice is the Grand Canal, the city's main waterway. You can ride a gondola along the canal and admire the beautiful buildings and bridges that line its banks.

The Rialto Bridge is another iconic landmark in Venice and is the oldest and most famous of the four bridges that cross the Grand Canal. It's a popular spot for taking photos and enjoying the view of the canal.

Venice is also known for its art and museums. The Peggy Guggenheim Collection is a modern art museum in the Palazzo Venier dei Leoni and features works by artists like Salvador Dali and Jackson Pollock. The Gallerie dell'Accademia is another important museum in Venice and houses a Renaissance art collection.

When it comes to food, Venice has a unique cuisine that features seafood and traditional Venetian dishes. Some must-try dishes include sarde in saor (marinated sardines), risotto al nero di seppia (squid ink risotto), and fegato alla veneziana (Venetian-style liver and onions).

Venice is a beautiful and romantic city that offers a unique experience unlike any other city. Its stunning architecture, canals, and art make it a must-visit location for anyone traveling to Italy.

Venice is a city full of beauty and charm; there's always something new and exciting to discover here. Whether exploring the city's canals and architecture or soaking up its art and culture, Venice will surely leave you enchanted and inspired.

Venice is a unique and beautiful city known for its stunning canals, architecture, and rich history. Here

are some more things to see and do when visiting
Venice:

THE PIAZZA SAN MARCO

The Piazza San Marco, known as St. Mark's Square, is the heart of Venice and is home to the iconic St. Mark's Basilica, the Doge's Palace, and several cafes and shops. The square is particularly beautiful in the early morning before the crowds arrive.

The square is surrounded by stunning architecture, including St. Mark's Basilica, the Doge's Palace, and the Procuratie Vecchie and Nuove.

Visitors to the Piazza San Marco can enjoy various activities, including walking around the square to take in the architecture, visiting the nearby museums and galleries, and dining in one of the many cafes and restaurants. There are also often live music performances and other events in the square.

One of the most popular activities in the Piazza San Marco is feeding the pigeons, which are plentiful in the area. Visitors can purchase birdseed from vendors in the square to feed the pigeons, although this practice has been discouraged in recent years due to concerns about the health and safety of both the pigeons and the visitors.

Overall, the Piazza San Marco is a must-visit destination for anyone traveling to Venice, and it provides a perfect introduction to the history and beauty of the city.

ST. MARK'S BASILICA

St. Mark's Basilica, also known as the Basilica di San Marco, is one of the most famous churches in Venice, Italy. It is located in St. Mark's Square and has distinctive Byzantine architecture. The basilica was originally built in the 9th century to house the remains of St. Mark, the patron saint of Venice.

The basilica's exterior is covered in intricate mosaics, and the main entrance features five large arches. Inside, the basilica is decorated with ornate marble and gold leaf and features numerous works of art, including mosaics, sculptures, and paintings.

The most impressive features of the basilica are the Pala d'Oro, a golden altarpiece that dates back to the 11th century. It is decorated with over 1,900 precious stones and is considered one of Venice's most valuable and important art pieces.

St. Mark's Basilica visitors can take a guided tour to learn more about its history and art or explore independently with an audio guide. Dressing modestly when visiting the basilica is recommended, as it is a place of worship. St. Mark's Basilica is a must-visit attraction in Venice, Italy. This beautiful cathedral is a prime example of Venetian architecture in Piazza San Marco.

The basilica is famous for its impressive mosaics covering almost the entire interior. These mosaics depict scenes from Jesus Christ's life and Venice's history.

Visitors can also marvel at the golden altarpiece and the marble floors.

One of the highlights of visiting St. Mark's Basilica is ascending to the terrace, where you can enjoy panoramic views of Venice and the surrounding lagoon. The famous Campanile, bell tower, and the Doge's Palace are here.

It's important to note that St. Mark's Basilica is a religious site, so visitors are expected to dress appropriately and behave respectfully. This means no shorts, short skirts, or bare shoulders. Additionally, visitors are not allowed to take photos inside the basilica.

Entry to St. Mark's Basilica is free, but there is a fee to access the terrace.

THE DOGE'S PALACE

This impressive Gothic palace was the residence of the Doge of Venice, the city's ruler, and is now a museum. Visitors can explore the palace's ornate rooms and learn about its fascinating history.

The Doge's Palace is a stunning palace located in Venice, Italy. It was once the Doge of Venice's residence, the Venetian Republic's supreme authority. Today, it is a popular tourist attraction that offers visitors a glimpse into the wealthy lifestyle of Venetian rulers.

The palace is a beautiful example of Venetian Gothic architecture, adorned with intricate carvings and stunning paintings. Visitors can explore the palace's many rooms, including the famous Golden Staircase, which the Doge used for important ceremonies.

One of the highlights of a visit to the Doge's Palace is crossing the Bridge of Sighs, a beautiful enclosed bridge that connects the palace to the prison. Myth has it that the bridge earned its name because it was prisoners' last glimpse of the beautiful city before they were taken to their cells.

The Doge's Palace is also home to several museums, including the Museo dell'Opera, which houses the palace's original artworks and furnishings, and the Museo Correr, which features Venetian history and culture.

Visitors should plan to spend several hours exploring the Doge's Palace to appreciate its beauty and history fully. It is recommended to buy tickets in advance to avoid long lines, especially during peak tourist season.

THE PEGGY GUGGENHEIM COLLECTION

Peggy Guggenheim Collection houses a collection of modern art, including works by Picasso, Dalí, and Pollock. The museum is in the Palazzo Venier dei Leoni, a historic building overlooking the Grand Canal.

The Peggy Guggenheim Collection is a modern art museum in Venice, Italy. It is housed in the Palazzo Venier dei Leoni, a beautiful 18th-century palace once home to Peggy Guggenheim, an American art collector, and socialite. The museum's collection features works by prominent modern artists such as

Pablo Picasso, Salvador Dalí, Jackson Pollock, and many others.

Visitors to the museum can explore its many galleries and exhibitions, which showcase a wide range of artistic movements and styles from the 20th century. The museum also hosts a series of temporary exhibitions, concerts, and cultural events throughout the year.

The museum is located on the Grand Canal, near the Accademia bridge, and is easily accessible by vaporetto or water taxi. It is open every day except Tuesday, from 10:00 am to 6:00 pm, and admission fees apply. Visitors can buy tickets online or at the museum's ticket office.

LA FENICE THEATRE

La Fenice Theatre, located in Venice, is one of Italy's most famous and iconic opera houses. The original theater was built in 1792 but has been rebuilt many times over the years due to fires and other incidents.

This historic opera house has been restored multiple times, most recently after a devastating fire in 1996. Visitors can take a guided theatre tour to learn about its history and architecture.

The theater has a rich history, hosting performances by some of the greatest opera singers and composers, including Gioachino Rossini, Vincenzo Bellini,

Giuseppe Verdi, and Richard Wagner. In addition to opera, La Fenice also hosts concerts and ballet performances.

Visitors can take guided theater tours to learn more about its history and architecture. The tour includes access to the theater's various halls and rooms and a visit to the museum, which contains various objects and artifacts related to the theater's history.

THE GALLERIE
DELL'ACCADEMIA

This museum is home to an impressive collection of Venetian art, including works by famous artists like Bellini, Titian, and Tintoretto. The museum is located in the Dorsoduro neighborhood, near the Accademia Bridge. The Gallerie dell'Accademia is a museum in the Dorsoduro district of Venice, Italy. The museum is renowned for its collection of pre-19th-century Venetian art, with works by artists such as Giovanni Bellini, Giorgione, Titian, and Tintoretto.

The Gallerie dell'Accademia was originally founded in the 18th century as an art school, but it later became a museum to showcase works by Venetian artists. The collection features many religious works, portraits, landscapes, and a notable Renaissance collection. Some of the most famous works on display include Bellini's "St. Francis in Ecstasy," Giorgione's "The Tempest," Titian's "Pieta," and Tintoretto's "Crucifixion."

The museum is housed in the Scuola della Carità, a former convent built in the 14th century. Visitors can tour the various rooms of the museum to see the many paintings, sculptures, and other works on display.

The museum also hosts temporary exhibitions and educational programs for visitors of all ages.

THE SCUOLA GRANDE DI SAN ROCCO

This 16th-century building is home to a stunning collection of paintings by Tintoretto, one of Venice's most famous artists. The paintings cover the walls and ceilings of the building's main hall and are breathtaking.

This ornate building was originally a religious confraternity and now houses a museum featuring works by Tintoretto. The interior of the building is covered in intricate frescoes and decorations. Scuola Grande di San Rocco is a stunning 16th-century building in Venice, Italy. It was founded as a charitable institution in 1478 and was rebuilt after a fire in 1517. The building is known for its incredible collection of paintings by Tintoretto, a famous Venetian artist.

Scuola Grande di San Rocco is a must-see for art lovers visiting Venice. The building is a work of art with beautiful architecture and stunning interiors. The highlight of the visit is the collection of paintings by Tintoretto, which covers the walls and ceilings of the main hall.

The Scuola Grande di San Rocco is open to the public daily from 9:30 am to 5:30 pm, and admission costs €10 for adults. It's recommended to book tickets in advance to avoid long queues. Guided tours are also available for those who want to learn more about the history and art of the building.

GRAND CANAL

The Grand Canal is the main waterway in Venice, Italy, and it's one of the most iconic landmarks in the city. The canal is about 3.8 km long and winds through the city, connecting the lagoon to the Santa Lucia railway station. The Grand Canal has more than 170 beautiful historic buildings, including palaces, churches, and museums.

One of the best ways to experience the Grand Canal is to take a water taxi or a gondola ride. From the water, you can see the beautiful facades of the buildings, including the famous Rialto Bridge, which crosses the canal at its narrowest point. Along the way, you'll also see several historic churches, including the Church of Santa Maria della Salute, built in the 17th century as a thanksgiving for the end of the plague in Venice.

Another great way to see the Grand Canal is to take a vaporetto, a water bus running up and down the canal. This is a more affordable option than a water taxi or gondola ride, and it's a great way to get a sense of the scale of the canal and see the different neighborhoods along its banks. Some of the most popular vaporetto routes include Line 1, which runs the length of the Grand Canal, and Line 2, which takes you through the quieter back canals of the city.

The Grand Canal has several important landmarks and buildings, including the Rialto Bridge. The bridge spans the Grand Canal and is a common spot for tourists to take photos and enjoy the views.

Along the Grand Canal, visitors can also see numerous palaces and churches that showcase Venice's architectural and artistic beauty. Some notable buildings include Ca' d'Oro, a Gothic-style palace that now serves as an art museum; Palazzo Barbarigo, a Renaissance-era palace with ornate façades; and Santa Maria della Salute, a magnificent baroque church with a dome that dominates the Venetian skyline.

One of the best ways to experience the Grand Canal is by taking a water taxi or Vaporetto, a water bus running up and down the canal, making stops at various points of interest. Visitors can also take a gondola ride, which offers a more intimate and romantic way to see the canal and its surroundings.

THE RIALTO BRIDGE

Rialto Bridge is one of the most photographed landmarks in Venice. Built in the 16th century, it spans the Grand Canal and is lined with shops and restaurants. The Rialto Bridge is a well-known landmark in Venice in the city's heart.

The bridge spans the Grand Canal and connects the San Marco and San Polo districts. It is one of the most beautiful bridges in Venice and a popular destination for tourists.

The bridge was built in the late 16th century and was the first permanent bridge built across the Grand Canal, and it replaced a wooden bridge that had been in place since the 12th century. The Rialto Bridge is made of white Istrian stone and has two inclined ramps leading up to a central portico. The portico has shops selling souvenirs, jewelry, and other merchandise.

The Rialto Bridge is a popular spot for taking photographs of the Grand Canal and the surrounding area. Visitors can also take a gondola ride under the bridge and admire its unique architecture from below. The bridge is also a popular meeting place for locals and tourists alike, and there are many cafes and restaurants in the area where visitors can relax and enjoy the view.

THE ISLANDS

Venice is situated on small Venetian Lagoon islands connected to the Adriatic Sea. There are over 100 islands in the Venetian Lagoon, but only a few are inhabited. Some of the most popular islands to visit from Venice include Murano, known for its glassblowing traditions; Burano, famous for its brightly colored houses and lace-making; and Torcello, which has a beautiful cathedral and is home to only a few residents.

Venice is surrounded by several small islands, each with its unique charm. You can take a boat tour to the islands of Murano, known for its glassblowing, and Burano, famous for its colorful houses and lace-making.

Known for its glass-making industry, Murano is home to many glass factories and studios where visitors can watch artisans create beautiful glass sculptures.

Murano, one of the islands near Venice, is famous for its glassblowing tradition. You can watch glassblowers at work in their studios or even take a glassblowing workshop to create your unique souvenir.

Famous for its colorful houses and lace-making tradition, Burano is a popular spot for photography enthusiasts and those interested in traditional crafts.

Burano Island is known for its colorful houses and lace-making tradition. Burano is a small island located about 7 km from Venice. Visitors can take a water taxi or ferry to the island to explore its narrow streets and picturesque canals.

A long, narrow island that separates the Venetian Lagoon from the Adriatic Sea, Lido is a popular beach destination and is home to the Venice Film Festival.

Venice Lido is a long, narrow island home to some of the most common beaches in Venice. Visitors can rent a bike or stroll along the promenade to enjoy the sea views and architecture.

San Giorgio Maggiore is a small island located opposite St. Mark's Square and is home to a beautiful church and bell tower designed by Andrea Palladio. Visitors can climb the bell tower for panoramic views of Venice.

This island is home to the beautiful San Giorgio Maggiore church, which features a stunning bell tower with panoramic views of Venice.

Torcello is one of the oldest settlements in the Venetian Lagoon. Torcello is home to the Cathedral of Santa Maria Assunta, which features stunning Byzantine mosaics.

Known as the "Island of the Dead," San Michele is where many Venetians are buried, including famous figures such as Igor Stravinsky and Joseph Brodsky.

Located just across the canal from the main island of Venice, Giudecca is home to several luxury hotels and is known for its quiet, residential atmosphere.

EXPLORE THE BACKSTREETS

Venice is full of hidden alleys and canals, and exploring these quiet backstreets is a great way to discover the city's hidden gems. You'll find charming cafes, artisan workshops, and beautiful architecture tucked away in these hidden corners.

Exploring Venice's hidden alleys and canals is a wonderful way to discover the city's hidden gems and experience its unique charm. There are many picturesque neighborhoods to explore, such as Cannaregio, Castello, Dorsoduro, and San Polo, each with its character and attractions. You can wander down narrow alleyways and over small bridges, admiring the colorful buildings and stunning architecture. And don't forget to stop at one of the many charming cafes or wine bars for a refreshing drink or delicious snack!

Venice is renowned for its winding canals, but its hidden alleys and narrow passageways are equally fascinating. These quiet backstreets are where you can discover the city's hidden gems away from the crowds of tourists.

Venice's most charming hidden alleys include the Calle del Paradiso, a narrow street lined with historic buildings, and the Calle Varisco, a picturesque alleyway leading to the Campo San Polo.

One of the best ways to explore Venice's hidden alleys and canals is by getting lost and wandering off the main tourist routes. This can lead you to discover charming cafes, artisan workshops, and beautiful architecture tucked away in these hidden corners.

Overall, exploring Venice's hidden alleys and canals is a must-do activity for anyone visiting the city, allowing you to discover its authentic charm and unique character.

THE JEWISH GHETTO

Venice's Jewish Ghetto is the oldest in Europe, and exploring this historic neighborhood is a great way to learn about the city's Jewish history and culture. You'll find beautiful synagogues, kosher bakeries, and shops selling Jewish artifacts and souvenirs.

Visitors can learn about Venice's Jewish history and explore the area's synagogues and museums. The Jewish Ghetto is known for its traditional Jewish cuisine, including matzo ball soup and fried artichokes.

The Jewish Ghetto is another area in Venice that is worth exploring. The area has a distinct cultural and architectural character, with narrow streets and old buildings that witness the Jewish community's long history in Venice.

Venice's Jewish Ghetto is another hidden gem worth exploring. Located in the Cannaregio district, it is one of the oldest Jewish ghettos in the world, established in the 16th century.

The Republic of Venice established it to confine and segregate the Jewish population to a specific city area. Despite the initial restrictions placed upon the Jews, the community thrived and became an important center of Jewish culture and commerce.

Today, the Jewish Ghetto is a fascinating neighborhood to explore, with its winding streets and historic buildings. The area has several synagogues, a Jewish museum, and a kosher bakery. Visitors can also sample traditional Jewish-Italian dishes at many restaurants and cafes in the area.

One of the highlights of the Jewish Ghetto is the Campo del Ghetto Nuovo, a large square surrounded by elegant buildings that served as the center of the community. Another interesting site is the Fontego dei Tedeschi, a 16th-century building once a center of commerce for the German community in Venice.

Exploring the Jewish Ghetto is a great way to learn more about Venice's history and culture and see a different side of the city.

Florence

Florence is the capital city of the Tuscany region of Italy and is known for its stunning art and architecture, delicious food, and beautiful countryside. When visiting Florence, you must see Michelangelo's David statue, the Florence Cathedral, and the Uffizi Gallery.

One of the most famous landmarks in Florence is the Florence Cathedral, also known as the Duomo, a stunning cathedral that's an iconic symbol of the city. It's famous for its dome, designed by Filippo

Brunelleschi, a remarkable feat of engineering at the time.

Another must-visit attraction in Florence is the Uffizi Gallery, one of the world's oldest and most famous art museums. It's home to a vast collection of Renaissance art, including works by Michelangelo, Leonardo da Vinci, and Botticelli.

One of the most famous sculptures in the world, Michelangelo's David, is located in Florence at the Accademia Gallery. This stunning statue is a masterpiece of Renaissance art and is considered one of the most iconic works of art in history.

Michelangelo created the statue in the early 16th century. It was commissioned by the city of Florence to be placed on the roofline of the Florence Cathedral. Still, it was ultimately placed in front of the Palazzo della Signoria, the seat of government in Florence.

Florence is also known for its delicious cuisine, including dishes like bistecca alla Fiorentina (a

Florentine-style steak), ribollita (a hearty vegetable soup), and pappa al pomodoro (a tomato and bread soup).

Florence is surrounded by beautiful Tuscan countryside, including the Chianti wine region, home to some of the best vineyards in Italy. It's the perfect place to take a scenic drive, enjoy a wine tasting, or explore the picturesque towns and villages in the area.

Tuscany is known for its delicious cuisine, a great way to learn more about the region's food and culture. You can learn how to make classic Tuscan dishes like pasta, bruschetta, and tiramisu and even visit a local market to buy ingredients.

Florence is a city full of art, history, delicious food, and stunning countryside. It's a must-visit destination for those interested in Renaissance art and architecture and those looking to experience the best Italian culture and cuisine.

Florence is a city full of beauty and history; there's always something new and exciting to discover here. Whether exploring the city's art and architecture or enjoying its delicious cuisine and beautiful gardens, Florence will surely leave you enchanted and inspired.

Florence is a city full of history, culture, and natural beauty, and there's always something new and exciting to discover here. Whether exploring the city's famous landmarks or taking a day trip to the Tuscan countryside, Florence will leave you with lasting memories.

Florence is a city full of surprises, and there are plenty of other things to see and do when you visit. Florence is a beautiful city in the heart of Tuscany, and it's known for its rich history, stunning architecture, and incredible art.

In the next section are some more things to see and do when visiting Florence:

MICHELANGELO'S DAVID STATUE

Michelangelo's David statue is a masterpiece of Renaissance art and a symbol of Florence, Italy. The statue is located in the Accademia Gallery in Florence and considered one of the greatest masterpieces ever.

Michelangelo created the David statue between 1501 and 1504, depicting the biblical hero David standing over the head of the slain Goliath. The statue stands 17 feet tall and is made entirely of marble. The statue was originally intended to be placed on the roof of the Florence Cathedral, but it was eventually placed in the Piazza della Signoria, where a replica now stands.

The statue is over 17 feet tall and depicts the biblical hero David, who defeated the giant Goliath with a stone from his sling. David is shown standing with his sling over his left shoulder and his right foot on the head of the slain giant.

The statue is known for its incredible detail and realism. Michelangelo spent more than two years creating the statue out of a single block of marble. He worked tirelessly to capture the beauty of the human form, and David's muscular physique and intense gaze are considered some of the most impressive aspects of the sculpture.

Today, the statue is housed in the Accademia Gallery in Florence, where visitors can admire its beauty up close. It remains one of Florence's most popular tourist attractions and a must-see for art lovers visiting Italy.

Visitors can admire the David statue in the Accademia Gallery, housed in a specially designed room. The museum also features other works by Michelangelo, including the unfinished enslaved people and the magnificent sculpture of Saint Matthew.

THE FLORENCE CATHEDRAL

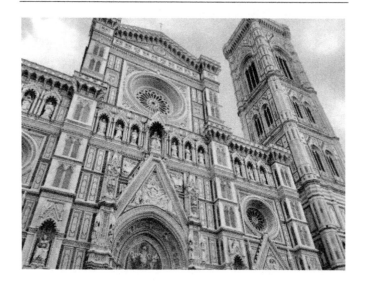

The Florence Cathedral, also known as the Duomo, is one of the city's most iconic landmarks. The cathedral's dome is an engineering marvel, and climbing to the top offers stunning city views.

The Florence Cathedral, also known as the Cathedral of Santa Maria del Fiore, is a famous landmark in Florence, Italy. The cathedral is an iconic example of Gothic and Renaissance architecture and features the famous dome designed by Filippo Brunelleschi.

The cathedral began in 1296 and took over 140 years to complete. The cathedral's exterior is decorated with intricate marble panels and statues, while the interior is adorned with frescoes and stained glass windows.

Visitors can climb to the top of the dome for stunning panoramic views of Florence.

The cathedral is located in the heart of Florence and is easily accessible by public transportation or on foot. Visitors should know that a strict dress code for entering the cathedral requires covering shoulders and legs. Additionally, tickets must be purchased in advance for the dome climb and other attractions within the cathedral complex.

THE UFFIZI GALLERY.

The Uffizi Gallery is a prominent art museum located in Florence, Italy. It is one of the world's most famous and oldest art museums, founded in 1581 by the Grand Duke of Tuscany, Francesco I de' Medici. The museum houses an incredible art collection from the Middle Ages to the Modern Period.

Visitors can admire works by some of the most famous artists in history, including Leonardo da Vinci, Michelangelo, Raphael, Caravaggio, and Botticelli. The museum also features a large collection of ancient Roman and Greek sculptures and a vast collection of paintings and drawings from the Renaissance period.

The Uffizi Gallery has several sections, each with its unique art collection. The museum's most famous artwork is Botticelli's "The Birth of Venus," but there are many other masterpieces to be discovered, including Michelangelo's "Doni Tondo" and Caravaggio's "Medusa."

Due to its popularity, the Uffizi Gallery can get quite busy, especially during peak tourist season. It is highly recommended to book tickets in advance to avoid waiting in long lines. The museum also offers guided tours for visitors who want a more in-depth experience and understanding of the artwork.

THE PONTE VECCHIO

This famous bridge spans the Arno River and has shops selling jewelry and other souvenirs. The bridge offers beautiful views of the river and the city, particularly at sunset.

The Ponte Vecchio is a famous bridge in Florence, Italy. It spans the Arno River and is known for its shops that sell jewelry, art, and other souvenirs. The bridge dates back to the 14th century and has a long and fascinating history.

Originally, the Ponte Vecchio was lined with butcher shops and fishmongers, as it was common to dispose of the waste directly into the river.

However, in 1593, the Medici Grand Duke Ferdinand I ordered that the shops be replaced with goldsmiths and jewelers, which the bridge is still known for today.

During World War II, the Ponte Vecchio was the only bridge in Florence that the Germans did not destroy as they retreated from the city. It is said that Hitler had ordered that the bridge be spared because of its beauty.

Today, the Ponte Vecchio is a popular tourist attraction and a symbol of Florence. Visitors can stroll across the bridge, admire the view of the river, and shop for souvenirs in the many jewelry stores.

THE PITTI PALACE

This impressive palace was the residence of the Medici family, one of the most powerful families in Florence's history. The palace is now home to several museums, including the Palatine Gallery, which houses a Renaissance art collection.

The Pitti Palace is a massive Renaissance palace located on the south side of the Arno River in Florence, Italy. It was originally built for a wealthy Florentine banker named Luca Pitti in the 15th century, but it was later acquired by the Medici family and used as their main residence.

Today, the Pitti Palace houses several museums, including the Palatine Gallery, the Royal Apartments, the Silver Museum, the Costume Gallery, and the Modern Art Gallery. The Palatine Gallery features a vast collection of Renaissance art, including works by Raphael, Titian, and Rubens. The Royal Apartments are decorated in a lavish Baroque style and feature frescoes, tapestries, and other decorative arts. The Silver Museum contains an extensive collection of decorative objects made from precious metals, including gold and silver tableware, cups, and caskets. The Costume Gallery features a collection of historic fashion from the 18th to the 20th century. Finally, the Modern Art Gallery displays art from the late 18th century to the 1930s, including pieces by Italian artists such as Giorgio Morandi and Felice Casorati.

In addition to its impressive art collections, the Pitti Palace is renowned for its extensive gardens, covering over 110 acres and featuring fountains, statues, and various plant species. The Boboli Gardens, part of the palace complex, offer spectacular views of Florence and the surrounding countryside. The gardens also feature numerous sculptures, including works by Michelangelo and Giambologna.

Overall, the Pitti Palace is a must-see destination for anyone interested in art and architecture. Its rich history and stunning collections offer visitors a glimpse into the opulent world of the Medici family and the grandeur of the Renaissance era.

THE BOBOLI GARDENS

These beautiful gardens are behind the Pitti Palace and offer stunning city views. The gardens are filled with sculptures, fountains, and beautiful plants and are a great place to relax and unwind.

The Boboli Gardens is a historic park in Florence that covers over 111 acres behind the Pitti Palace. It was designed for the Medici family in the 16th century and is considered one of the finest examples of Italian-style gardens worldwide.

Visitors to the Boboli Gardens can enjoy a peaceful escape from the busy city streets and explore the park's many paths, fountains, sculptures, and botanical treasures. Several highlights include the Amphitheatre, designed to host outdoor performances, and the Isolotto, a small island with a fountain.

Other popular features of the gardens include the Grotta Grande, a cave-like structure with colorful frescoes and shell-shaped decorations, and the Kaffeehaus, a pavilion built in the 18th century that serves refreshments.

The Boboli Gardens is open to visitors every day except for the first and last Monday of the month, and tickets can be purchased on-site or online in advance. Guided tours are also available for those who want to learn more about the history and design of the gardens.

THE BASILICA OF SANTA CROCE

This beautiful church is the final resting place of some of Florence's most famous citizens, including Michelangelo, Galileo, and Machiavelli. The church's interior is filled with stunning art and architecture, including frescoes by Giotto.

The Basilica of Santa Croce is one of the most important churches in Florence. It is often called the "Temple of the Italian Glories" due to its many tombs and monuments dedicated to famous Italians. The church is located in the Piazza Santa Croce and is a beautiful example of Italian Gothic architecture.

The Basilica of Santa Croce was built in the 13th century and has since undergone several renovations and expansions. The church's interior is filled with beautiful works of art and frescoes, including some by Giotto and his followers. Many tombs and memorials are dedicated to some of the most famous Italians in history, including Galileo Galilei, Michelangelo, and Dante Alighieri.

Visitors to the Basilica of Santa Croce can take a guided tour to learn more about the history and art of the church or wander through the beautiful interior on their own. The church is open daily to visitors, although there may be some restrictions during religious services or events.

THE SAN LORENZO MARKET

This bustling market is great for souvenirs, leather goods, and traditional Tuscan foods. You'll find everything from fresh produce and cheese to handmade ceramics and jewelry.

The San Lorenzo Market is a vibrant outdoor marketplace in the heart of Florence, Italy. The market has been a staple of the city since the 19th century and is known for its lively atmosphere, colorful stalls, and a wide variety of products.

Visitors to the San Lorenzo Market can browse various goods, from fresh produce and artisanal cheeses to handmade leather goods and souvenirs. The market is also home to several small cafes and eateries, offering a chance to rest and enjoy a coffee or a traditional Tuscan meal.

One of the highlights of the San Lorenzo Market is the Central Market, a large indoor food hall that features some of the best local produce and gourmet specialties. Here, visitors can sample fresh pasta, local cheeses, and meats and even indulge in wine tasting.

Whether you're searching for fresh ingredients for a home-cooked meal or looking for a unique souvenir to take home, the San Lorenzo Market is a must-visit destination in Florence.

THE TUSCAN COUNTRYSIDE.

The hills and vineyards of Tuscany are some of the most beautiful in Italy, and taking a day trip to the countryside is a great way to experience the region's natural beauty. You can visit charming medieval towns like San Gimignano or explore the famous Chianti wine region.

The Tuscan countryside is a beautiful and picturesque central Italy region known for its rolling hills, vineyards, and charming towns.

Here are some travel tips for exploring this region:

Rent a car: The best way to explore the Tuscan countryside is by car. You can rent a car in Florence or Pisa and drive leisurely through the countryside, stopping at charming towns.

Visit the hill towns: The Tuscan countryside is dotted with beautiful hill towns, such as San Gimignano, Montepulciano, and Volterra. These towns are known for their historic architecture, beautiful views, and delicious local cuisine.

Sample the local wine: Tuscany is known for its wine, and there are many vineyards in the countryside where you can sample the local vintages. Some of the most famous wines from the region include Chianti, Brunello di Montalcino, and Vino Nobile di Montepulciano.

Go on a bike tour: If you're looking for a more active way to explore the countryside, consider going on a bike tour. Many companies offer guided bike tours through the Tuscan countryside, where you can enjoy the beautiful scenery and fresh air while getting some exercise.

Visit the thermal baths: Tuscany is also known for its thermal baths, which have healing properties. Many thermal baths are throughout the region, including the famous baths in Bagno Vignoni and Saturnia.

Enjoy the food: Tuscan cuisine is known for its simplicity and use of fresh, local ingredients. Be sure to try some of the local specialties, such as ribollita (a hearty vegetable soup), pappa al pomodoro (a tomato and bread soup), and bistecca alla Fiorentina (a thick, juicy steak).

THE BARGELLO MUSEUM

This museum is home to a stunning collection of Renaissance art and sculpture, including works by Michelangelo and Donatello. The museum is located in a beautiful medieval palace and is a must-visit for art lovers.

The Bargello Museum is in Florence, Italy, home to one of the most important collections of Italian Renaissance sculpture. It is located in the Palazzo del Bargello, a historic building built as a fortress in the 13th century.

The museum's collection includes works by some of the greatest artists of the Renaissance, including Michelangelo, Donatello, and Cellini. Among the collection's highlights are Michelangelo's Bacchus, Donatello's David, and the bronze reliefs from Ghiberti's Gates of Paradise.

In addition to its impressive sculpture collection, the Bargello Museum also houses a large collection of decorative arts, including ceramics, tapestries, and textiles. The museum's courtyard is also home to a collection of 16th-century bronze sculptures.

Visitors to the Bargello Museum can explore its many galleries and rooms, filled with beautiful works of art. Audio guides are available to provide additional information about the museum's collection.

Overall, the Bargello Museum is a must-visit destination for anyone interested in Renaissance art and sculpture. Its collection is unparalleled, and the museum is a beautiful example of Renaissance architecture.

THE SUNSET FROM PIAZZALE MICHELANGELO

This scenic overlook offers stunning views of Florence and is a popular sunset spot. You can take a bus or walk up to the overlook, and there are several restaurants and cafes nearby where you can enjoy a meal or a drink.

The Sunset from Piazzale Michelangelo is a must-see attraction in Florence. This stunning panoramic viewpoint offers breathtaking views of the city and the surrounding hills. You can watch the sunset while enjoying a glass of wine and local delicacies from nearby vendors.

Piazzale Michelangelo is located on a hill above the city center and can be easily reached by foot, bike, or bus. The square is adorned with a bronze replica of Michelangelo's David statue, and it offers stunning views of the Arno River, the Duomo, and the surrounding hills.

The best time to visit Piazzale Michelangelo is in the late afternoon, just before sunset. This is when the sky's colors blend with the city's, creating a breathtaking and romantic atmosphere. It can get crowded during peak season, so arriving early is best to secure a good spot.

Naples

Naples is a vibrant city located in the Campania region of southern Italy. It's known for its incredible food, rich history, and stunning architecture.

Naples is a beautiful city located in the south of Italy, and it's known for its incredible food, architecture, and history. When visiting Naples, you should visit the Pompeii ruins, the Royal Palace of Naples, and the Naples National Archaeological Museum.

One of the most popular attractions in Naples is the Pompeii ruins, an ancient Roman city buried in volcanic ash after the eruption of Mount Vesuvius in 79 AD. It's now an open-air museum where you can see the remarkably preserved ruins of the city, including homes, shops, and public buildings.

Another must-see attraction in Naples is the Royal Palace of Naples, which was built in the 17th century and is one of the most impressive palaces in Italy. It's home to a vast collection of art, including works by Caravaggio, Titian, and Raphael.

The Naples National Archaeological Museum is also a must-visit destination for anyone interested in history and archaeology. It's home to an impressive collection of artifacts from Pompeii and other ancient Roman sites in the region.

Naples is also known for its incredible food, including pizza, which is said to have originated in the city. Many pizzerias in Naples serve up delicious, authentic Neapolitan pizza and other local specialties like spaghetti alle vongole (spaghetti with clams) and sfogliatelle (a pastry filled with sweet ricotta cheese).

Naples is known for its delicious food, and it's a great place to try classic Italian dishes like pizza, pasta, and seafood. You can visit local markets like the Mercato di Porta Nolana to sample fresh produce and other ingredients or try one of the city's many pizzerias or trattorias.

Naples is a great base for exploring the surrounding area, including the Amalfi Coast, Capri, and the islands of Ischia and Procida. These destinations are known for their beautiful beaches, stunning landscapes, and charming towns and villages.

Overall, Naples is a city full of history, culture, and delicious food. It's a must-visit destination for anyone interested in ancient Roman history and those looking to experience the best Italian cuisine and culture.

Naples is a city with a unique character and energy, and there's always something new and exciting to discover here. Whether exploring the city's history and culture or indulging in its delicious food and wine, Naples will leave you lasting memories.

Naples is a fascinating city with a rich history and a vibrant culture. Here are some more things to see and do when you visit:

THE POMPEII RUINS

The Pompeii ruins are an archaeological site located near Naples in southern Italy. The city of Pompeii was destroyed by the eruption of Mount Vesuvius in 79 AD and remained buried under layers of ash and pumice until its rediscovery in the 18th century.

Today, visitors can explore the ruins of Pompeii and get a glimpse of what life was like in ancient Roman times. Highlights of the site include the Amphitheater, the Forum, the Temple of Apollo, the House of the Faun, and the House of the Vettii. Many of the ruins are remarkably well-preserved, with intricate mosaics, frescoes, and other details that offer insight into the daily life and customs of the city's inhabitants.

Visitors can also see the casts of some of the eruption victims, made by pouring plaster into the cavities left by the decomposed bodies. The casts offer a haunting reminder of the tragedy that struck the city.

The Pompeii ruins can be visited on a day trip from Naples, Sorrento, or the Amalfi Coast. Guided tours are available, and visitors can also explore the site independently with the help of a guidebook or audio guide.

THE ROYAL PALACE OF NAPLES

The Royal Palace of Naples, also known as the Palazzo Reale, is stunning in the heart of Naples, Italy. The Spanish viceroy built it in the 17th century, and it was the royal residence of the Bourbon Kings of Naples during the 18th and 19th centuries.

The palace features a grand façade that overlooks the Piazza del Plebiscito and is adorned with beautiful statues and frescoes. Visitors can explore the royal apartments decorated with ornate furnishings, tapestries, and artwork.

One of the highlights of the Royal Palace is the Royal Chapel, which is decorated with beautiful frescoes and contains a collection of valuable religious artifacts. Visitors can also explore the palace's art collection, which includes works by some of Italy's most famous artists.

The palace also boasts a beautiful garden home to rare plants and trees. Visitors can stroll through the garden and enjoy the peaceful surroundings while taking in the beautiful views of Naples.

Overall, the Royal Palace of Naples is a must-see attraction for anyone visiting Naples. Its stunning architecture, beautiful artwork, and rich history make it one of the most important cultural landmarks in the city.

THE NAPLES NATIONAL ARCHAEOLOGICAL MUSEUM.

The Naples National Archaeological Museum is a must-visit for anyone interested in ancient history and archaeology. The museum is home to an extensive collection of ancient Greece and Rome artifacts, including sculptures, frescoes, and mosaics.

Some of the most famous exhibits in the museum include the Farnese Collection, a collection of sculptures from the ancient world that the Farnese family once owned, and the Secret Cabinet, a collection of erotic art and artifacts from Pompeii and Herculaneum.

Visitors can also see the treasures of ancient Pompeii, which were preserved by the volcanic eruption of Mount Vesuvius in AD 79. The museum features an impressive collection of frescoes, mosaics, and other artifacts from Pompeii, providing a glimpse into life in ancient Rome.

The Naples National Archaeological Museum is located in the heart of Naples and is easily accessible by public transportation. The museum is open daily except on Tuesdays, and tickets can be purchased online in advance or at the entrance on the day of your visit.

THE ISLANDS OF ISCHIA AND PROCIDA

Ischia and Procida are two beautiful islands in the Bay of Naples, not far from Naples. They are both great places to visit for a relaxing day trip or a longer stay.

Ischia is the larger of the two islands known for its thermal spas and stunning beaches. The island has a rich history and is home to several interesting archaeological sites, including the Aragonese Castle and the ancient Roman town of Aenaria.

Conversely, Procida is a small, charming island with colorful houses and narrow streets. It's a great place to explore on foot and has a laid-back atmosphere, perfect for a relaxing day by the sea.

Both islands are easily accessible by ferry from Naples or other nearby towns and offer a peaceful escape from the bustling city.

THE CASTEL DELL'OVO

This ancient castle is perched on a small island in the Bay of Naples, and it offers stunning views of the city and the sea. The castle's history dates back to Roman times, and it's now home to a museum and several restaurants.

The Castel dell'Ovo is a castle on a small island in the Gulf of Naples, off the coast of the city of Naples in Italy. It is one of the oldest fortifications in the city, and it has a rich history that dates back to the Roman era. The castle is located on the islet of Megaride, once the site of the original Greek settlement.

Castel dell'Ovo means "Castle of the Egg" in Italian, and it is believed to have derived from an ancient legend. According to the legend, the Roman poet Virgil placed a magical egg in the castle's foundations to protect it from destruction. If the egg were to break, the castle would be destroyed, and with it, the entire city of Naples.

Today, the castle is a popular tourist attraction in Naples, offering stunning views of the city and the Gulf of Naples. Visitors can explore the castle and its grounds, which include a museum and a small chapel. The museum houses a collection of ancient artifacts and artwork, including paintings, sculptures, and ceramics. In addition to its historical significance and cultural attractions, the Castel dell'Ovo is known for its excellent seafood restaurants. Many locals and tourists come to the castle to enjoy fresh seafood dishes and soak up the views of the Gulf of Naples.

THE CAPODIMONTE MUSEUM

This museum is housed in a beautiful palace on a hill overlooking the city, and it's home to a stunning collection of art and sculpture. The museum's highlights include works by Caravaggio, Titian, and Botticelli.

The Capodimonte Museum is an art museum located in Naples, Italy. It houses one of the world's largest collections of Italian paintings, including masterpieces by Raphael, Caravaggio, Titian, and many others. The museum is located in the former Bourbon Palace of Capodimonte, built in the 18th century as a hunting lodge for the Bourbon kings of Naples.

The museum's collection is spread over three floors and includes over 1,200 works of art, mostly from the 13th to the 18th centuries. Some of the highlights of the collection include Caravaggio's "The Flagellation of Christ," Raphael's "Madonna of the Rose," and Titian's "Danae."

In addition to its extensive collection of paintings, the museum houses collections of decorative arts, including ceramics, glass, and furniture. There is also a large collection of Neapolitan nativity scenes, a traditional art form in Naples.

The Capodimonte Museum is in Capodimonte Park, a large park with beautiful gardens and several historic buildings. The park offers a peaceful escape from the city and is a popular spot for picnics and walks. Visitors can also enjoy panoramic views of Naples from the park's hilltop location.

The Capodimonte Museum is a must-see destination for art lovers visiting Naples. Its impressive collection of Italian paintings and beautiful setting in the Capodimonte Park make it a unique and memorable experience.

THE AMALFI COAST

The Amalfi Coast is one of the most beautiful stretches of coastline in the world, and it's just a short drive from Naples. You can take a bus or hire a car to explore the charming towns and villages along the coast or swim in the crystal-clear waters of the Tyrrhenian Sea.

The Amalfi Coast is a beautiful coastal region in southern Italy, known for its beautiful beaches and stunning landscapes. When visiting the Amalfi Coast, you should visit the towns of Positano, Amalfi, and Ravello.

Naples' historic center is a UNESCO World Heritage Site, and it's filled with beautiful churches, palaces, and narrow streets lined with shops and cafes. You can explore the city on foot.

The Amalfi Coast is a stunningly beautiful stretch of coastline in the Campania region of southern Italy. It's a popular tourist destination known for its picturesque villages, rugged cliffs, and crystal-clear waters.

The Amalfi Coast is a UNESCO World Heritage site, attracting millions of yearly visitors.

The Amalfi Coast stretches along the southern side of the Sorrentine Peninsula, comprising several small towns and villages, including Positano, Amalfi, Ravello, Praiano, and Atrani. Each town has its unique charm and character, offering breathtaking views of the sea and the surrounding landscape.

One of the main attractions of the Amalfi Coast is its beaches. The coastline is dotted with small coves and bays, many of which have pebble or sandy beaches.

Some popular beaches include Spiaggia Grande in Positano, Marina Grande in Amalfi, and Marina di Praia in Praiano.

The Amalfi Coast is also known for its scenic drives, with the famous Amalfi Drive being one of the most spectacular. This winding road runs along the coastline from Sorrento to Salerno, offering breathtaking views of the sea and the rugged cliffs.

The Amalfi Coast is popular for outdoor activities like hiking and kayaking. The area has many hiking trails, including the famous Path of the Gods, which offers stunning coastline views. Kayaking is also popular, with many tour operators offering guided tours of the sea caves and caverns along the coast.

The Amalfi Coast is known for its delicious cuisine, focusing on fresh seafood, locally grown produce, and traditional dishes. Some of the local specialties include spaghetti alle vongole (spaghetti with clams), scialatielli ai frutti di mare (a seafood pasta dish), and limoncello (a lemon liqueur).

Overall, the Amalfi Coast is a must-visit destination for anyone traveling to Italy. Its stunning beauty, charming towns, and delicious cuisine make it a true gem of the Mediterranean.

The Amalfi Coast is one of Italy's most beautiful regions, and it's worth a visit. Here are some more suggestions for things to see and do on the Amalfi Coast:

Take a boat tour - One of the best ways to see the Amalfi Coast is from the water. Many boat tours will take you along the coast, past picturesque fishing villages, secluded coves, and rocky cliffs. Some tours even include stops for swimming and snorkeling.

Visit the town of Sorrento - Sorrento is a charming town on a cliff overlooking the Bay of Naples. It's known for its lemon groves, narrow streets, and beautiful sea views. You can stroll through the town's historic center, visit its museums and churches, and enjoy local cuisines.

Explore the Path of the Gods - The Path of the Gods is a hiking trail along the Amalfi Coast, offering stunning views of the sea and the surrounding landscape. The trail is about 7.5 miles long and takes 4-5 hours. It's a moderately challenging hike, but the views are well worth it.

Visit the town of Praiano - Praiano is a small town between Positano and Amalfi, known for its quiet beaches, colorful houses, and relaxed atmosphere. It's a great place to escape the crowds and enjoy peace.

Try the local cuisine - The Amalfi Coast is known for its delicious food, including fresh seafood, homemade pasta, and locally grown fruits and vegetables. Be sure to try some of the local specialties, like spaghetti alle vongole (spaghetti with clams), limoncello (a lemon liqueur), and sfogliatella (a pastry filled with ricotta cheese and candied fruit).

The Amalfi Coast is a stunningly beautiful region full of natural wonders, charming towns, and delicious food. Whether you're looking to relax on the beach, explore the local culture, or get active, there's something for everyone here.

THE CATACOMBS OF SAN GENNARO

These ancient underground tombs are a fascinating glimpse into Naples' early Christian history. The catacombs are home to the remains of many of the city's saints and martyrs and are a popular attraction for visitors.

The Catacombs of San Gennaro are an underground complex of tunnels and tombs in Naples, Italy. They are one of the most important archaeological sites in the city and provide a unique insight into the early Christian era in Naples. The catacombs were used from the 2nd to the 5th century AD as a burial ground for Christians, and they are named after Saint Gennaro, the patron saint of Naples.

The catacombs consist of three levels, located beneath the modern city of Naples. The first level is the oldest, containing the tombs of some of the earliest Christians in Naples. The second level was built in the 3rd century, containing more elaborate tombs and frescoes. The third level was built in the 4th century and is the largest of the three levels.

Visitors can explore the catacombs on a guided tour, which includes access to some of the most interesting tombs and frescoes. One of the highlights of the catacombs is the tomb of Saint Gennaro, located on the second level. The tomb is adorned with frescoes that depict scenes from the saint's life.

Visitors should know that the catacombs can be quite dark and narrow, so it is not recommended for people with claustrophobia or mobility issues. However, for those who can visit, the catacombs offer a unique glimpse into the early Christian history of Naples.

THE LUNGOMARE

The Lungomare is Naples' waterfront promenade, offering beautiful sea and city views. You can walk along the promenade and stop at one of the many cafes and restaurants along the way to enjoy a coffee or a meal.

The Lungomare is a beautiful seaside promenade in Naples that stretches for about 3 kilometers (1.8 miles) along the Bay of Naples. The promenade offers stunning views of the sea and the Vesuvius volcano and is a popular spot for a relaxing walk, jog, or bike ride.

Along the way, visitors can admire several landmarks and attractions, such as the Castel dell'Ovo, the Castel dell'Angelo, the Villa Comunale park, and the Santa Lucia district. The Lungomare also features several restaurants, cafes, and bars where visitors can enjoy traditional Neapolitan cuisine or sip a coffee or cocktail while enjoying the beautiful scenery.

The Lungomare is a perfect spot to watch the sunset or soak up the city's atmosphere. It's a great place for a romantic stroll or a family outing and is easily accessible from the city center by public transportation or on foot.

THE CASTEL NUOVO

This imposing castle was built in the 13th century and is one of Naples' most iconic landmarks. The castle has served as a royal palace, a prison, and a military barracks over the centuries, and it's now home to a museum and several exhibitions.

Castel Nuovo, also known as Maschio Angioino, is a medieval castle in the heart of Naples. It was built by the French king Charles I of Anjou in the 13th century and has since been an important symbol of the city's history and power.

The castle has a unique blend of Gothic and Renaissance architecture, and its distinctive five towers make it easily recognizable from afar. It served as a royal residence and fortress for many centuries, and today it is a popular tourist destination and cultural center.

Inside the castle, visitors can explore the Sala dei Baroni, a magnificent hall decorated with frescoes and used for banquets and ceremonies. The castle also houses the Museum of the Decorative Arts, which displays an impressive collection of furniture, ceramics, glassware, and tapestries from the 16th to the 19th century.

The castle is in Piazza Municipio, near the Port of Naples and the Molo Beverello ferry terminal. It is open to the public daily, and guided tours are available in Italian and English. The castle offers stunning views of the Bay of Naples, and the nearby Galleria Umberto I shopping arcade is a great place to grab a bite to eat or shop.

THE UNDERGROUND NAPLES

Beneath the city's streets is an ancient network of tunnels and caverns known as Napoli Sotterranea. You can tour the underground tunnels to learn about Naples' history and see some of the city's hidden treasures.

The underground Naples is an extensive network of tunnels, caverns, and passageways beneath the city's historic center. These underground spaces were created by the Greeks and expanded by the Romans for water, food storage, and religious purposes. Over the centuries, underground tunnels were used for various purposes, including as bomb shelters during World War II.

Today, visitors can explore some of the underground Naples on guided tours. The tours take visitors through the ancient tunnels and passageways, revealing hidden chapels, ancient cisterns, and even the remains of a Roman theater. One of the most popular sites on tour is the Catacombs of San Gennaro, which feature early Christian tombs and frescoes.

Exploring the underground Naples is a unique way to discover the city's hidden history and gain a new perspective on its ancient past. However, visitors should be prepared for the underground tunnels' damp and dark conditions and wear comfortable shoes and clothing suitable for the underground environment.

CAPRI

The beautiful island of Capri is just a short boat ride from Naples and a popular day trip destination. You can explore the island's charming town, swim in the clear blue waters of the Mediterranean, and visit the famous Blue Grotto.

Capri is a beautiful island in the Tyrrhenian Sea off the Sorrentine Peninsula in southern Italy. It is a popular tourist destination due to its natural beauty, upscale shopping, and vibrant nightlife.

Here are some of the top attractions on the island:

The Blue Grotto: The Blue Grotto is a sea cave on the island's north coast. The cave is famous for its stunning blue water, illuminated by sunlight that enters through an underwater opening. Visitors can access the cave by boat.

Villa Jovis: Villa Jovis is a Roman palace Emperor Tiberius built in the 1st century AD. The palace is on a cliff overlooking the sea and offers spectacular views of the island and the surrounding waters.

Anacapri: Anacapri is a charming town on the island's western side. It is known for its narrow streets, traditional architecture, and stunning sea views. Visitors can take a chairlift to the top of Mount Solaro for even more breathtaking views.

Faraglioni: The Faraglioni are three rock formations that rise from the sea off the island's southern coast. They are one of the most iconic sights on Capri and can be viewed from several vantage points around the island.

Marina Piccola: Marina Piccola is a picturesque beach on the island's southern coast. It is a popular spot for sunbathing, swimming, and snorkeling and offers stunning views of the Faraglioni.

Punta Carena Lighthouse: The Punta Carena Lighthouse is located on the island's western side and offers stunning views of the sea and the surrounding landscape. Visitors can climb to the top of the lighthouse for even better views.

Gardens of Augustus: The Gardens of Augustus are located in Capri and offer beautiful views of the sea and the Faraglioni. The gardens are known for their colorful flowers and well-manicured pathways.

Shopping: Capri is known for its upscale shopping, with many high-end fashion boutiques in Capri. Visitors can shop for designer clothing, jewelry, and other luxury items.

Nightlife: Capri is known for its vibrant nightlife, with many bars and clubs in Capri. Visitors can enjoy

live music, dancing, and drinks with stunning sea
views.

Essential Tips For First-Timers

Here are some essential tips for first-time travelers to Italy:

Plan your trip ahead of time: Italy is a popular tourist destination, and it's important to plan to avoid long lines and crowded tourist attractions, so it's essential to ensure you can see everything you want to see. Book accommodations, transportation, and tickets to popular attractions in advance.

Learn some Italian: Even though most Italians speak English, it's always a good idea to learn some basic Italian phrases to communicate with the locals. It's always appreciated when visitors try to speak the local language. Learning basic Italian phrases can make your trip more enjoyable and help you connect with the locals.

Dress appropriately: Italians take fashion seriously, so it's essential to dress appropriately when visiting churches, cathedrals, and other religious sites. Cover your shoulders and knees, and avoid wearing revealing clothing in public.

Use public transportation: Italian cities can be busy, and public transportation is often easier. Italy has a great public transportation system, and it's often the easiest and most affordable way to get around. Trains are a great way to travel between cities, and buses and subways are a great way to get around within cities.

Try the local food: Italy is known for its incredible food, so be sure to try some local dishes when you visit. Try the local specialties in each region you visit, and don't be afraid to ask locals for recommendations.

Be mindful of cultural differences: Italians have their customs and way of life, and it's important to be mindful of cultural differences when visiting. For example, Italians typically eat dinner later than in many other countries, and taking a siesta in the afternoon is common.

Be aware of pickpockets: Like in many popular tourist destinations, pickpocketing can be a problem in Italy. Be aware of your surroundings and keep your belongings close to you, especially in crowded areas.

Don't try to do too much: Italy has so much to offer, but it's important not to do too much in one trip. Focus on a few key destinations and take the time to explore and enjoy them.

Enjoy the slower pace of life: Italians are known for their relaxed way of life, and it's important to take the time to enjoy the slower pace of life in Italy. Sit in a cafe, enjoy an espresso, or stroll through a beautiful town or park.

Conclusion

These are just a few of the many things to see and do when visiting Italy. The country is full of surprises, and you're sure to discover something new and exciting around every corner.

A guided tour of Italy can be a great way to gain a deeper understanding of this fascinating landmark and the history of ancient Italy.

Italy is a beautiful country filled with incredible sights and sounds. When visiting Italy, visit top destinations like Rome, Venice, Florence, Naples, and the Amalfi Coast. Follow these essential tips for first-timers, and you'll have an unforgettable experience discovering the soul of Italy.

Printed in Great Britain
by Amazon

23252794R00099